My World of Science

MAGNETIC AND NON-MAGNETIC

Angela Royston

Heinemann
LIBRARY

www.heinemann.co.uk/library
Visit our website to find out more information about **Heinemann Library** books.

To order:
- ☎ Phone 44 (0) 1865 888066
- 🖹 Send a fax to 44 (0) 1865 314091
- 🖥 Visit the Heinemann Bookshop at www.heinemann.co.uk/library to browse our catalogue and order online.

First published in Great Britain by Heinemann Library, Halley Court, Jordan Hill, Oxford OX2 8EJ, part of Harcourt Education.

Heinemann is a registered trademark of Harcourt Education Ltd.

Editorial: Andrew Farrow and Dan Nunn
Design: Jo Hinton-Malivoire and
    Tinstar Design Limited (www.tinstar.co.uk)
Picture Research: Maria Joannou and Sally Smith
Production: Viv Hichens

Originated by Blenheim Colour Ltd
Printed and bound in China by
    South China Printing Company

ISBN 0 431 13748 X
07 06 05 04 03
10 9 8 7 6 5 4 3 2 1

British Library Cataloguing in Publication Data
Magnetic and non-magnetic. –
(My world of science)
1. Magnetic materials – Juvenile literature
I. Title
620.1'1297

A full catalogue record for this book is available from the British Library.

Acknowledgements
The publishers would like to thank the following for permission to reproduce photographs:
Aviation Picture Library p. **29**; Hardlines p. **25**; Network Photographers p. **17**; Trevor Clifford pp. **4**, **5**, **6**, **7**, **8**, **9**, **10**, **11**, **12**, **13**, **14**, **15**, **16**, **21**, **22**, **26**, **27**, **28**; Trip/H. Rogers p. **23**; Unknown p. **24**; Zul Mukhida pp. **18**, **19**, **20**.

Cover photograph reproduced with permission of Trevor Clifford.

Every effort has been made to contact copyright holders of any material reproduced in this book. Any omissions will be rectified in subsequent printings if notice is given to the publishers.

Contents

Any words appearing in the text in bold, **like this**,
are explained in the Glossary.

What does a magnet do?

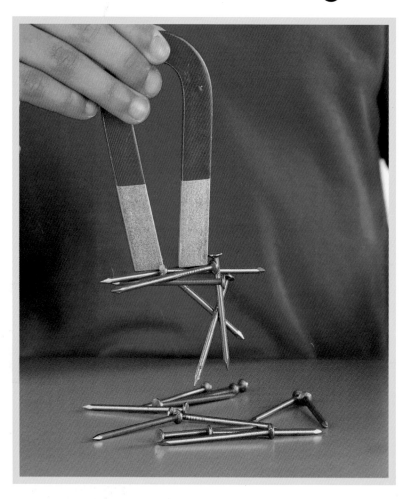

A magnet has the power to pull some things towards it. These nails have been pulled onto the magnet. The magnet's pull holds them there.

The magnet pulls the nail even when the magnet is not touching the nail. The power of this magnet lifts the nail into the air.

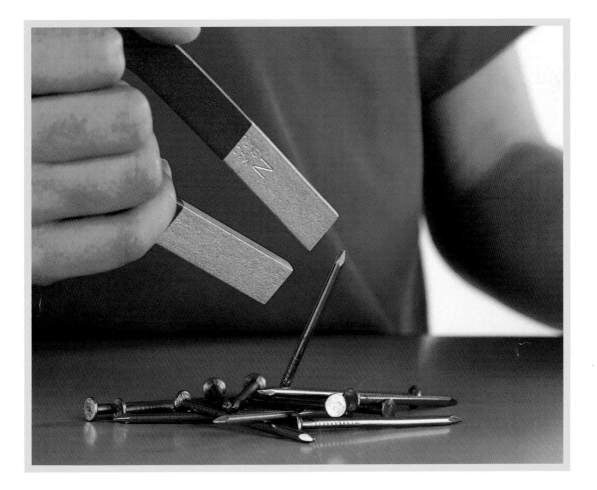

Magnetic materials

Only some kinds of materials are pulled towards a magnet. You can use a magnet to test which kinds of materials are pulled towards it.

All of these things were pulled
towards the magnet. They are all
made of iron or steel. Iron and
steel are said to be magnetic.

Are all metals magnetic?

These things are all made of metal. Only metal things can be magnetic, but not all metals are magnetic. Only iron and steel are magnetic.

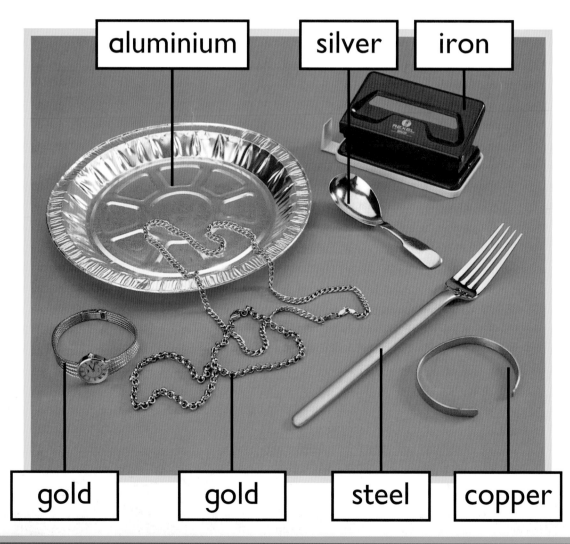

aluminium silver iron

gold gold steel copper

Some cans are made of **aluminium**. Others are made of steel. A magnet does not stick to aluminium. Which of these cans do you know is made of steel? (Answer on page 31.)

Non-magnetic materials

All of these materials are
non-magnetic. When you touch
them with a magnet, they do
not stick to the magnet.

This girl is sorting **paperclips** to find out which are magnetic and which are non-magnetic. The silver-coloured paperclips are made of steel. The rest are made of plastic. Which colours are non-magnetic? (Answer on page 31.)

Can magnetism pass through water?

This girl is testing to see if a magnet works in water. She puts the nail in a bowl of water. Then she brings the magnet close to it.

The nail jumps onto the magnet before the magnet touches it. So the pull of the magnet can pass through the water to the nail.

Can magnetism pass through other materials?

Cloth is non-magnetic, but the pull of the magnet passes through the cloth to the nail. Magnetism also works through paper and thin plastic.

Magnetism only passes through thin materials. These things are all too thick for the magnet to work through them. Its pull is not strong enough.

Using magnets

Many keys are made of steel, so they are magnetic. This key-holder is a long, thin magnet. The keys stick to it, so they should never get lost!

This cat has a magnet on her **collar**. The magnet releases a catch on her cat flap when she pushes it from the outside. No other cat can get in.

Magnets in toys

The **wagons** on this train are joined by magnets. The magnet on the front of one wagon sticks to the magnet on the back of the next wagon.

This travel game uses magnets to keep the pieces on the board. This means that you can play it in a moving car or on a train.

Magnets and fridges

Magnets stick to **refrigerators** because refrigerators are made of steel. You can use a magnet to stick a photograph to the door of a refrigerator.

A refrigerator door has a **rubber** strip around the edge. Below the rubber is a magnetic strip. The magnet sticks to the door to keep it tightly closed.

Magnetic rocks

This rock is called fool's gold. It looks like **gold**, but it contains iron, not gold. Certain kinds of rock that contain iron are magnetic.

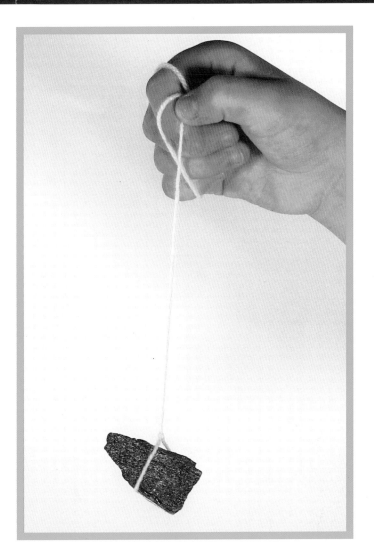

Lodestone is a natural magnet. It attracts things made of iron and steel. Hundreds of years ago people used lodestone to make simple **compasses**.

The Earth is a magnet

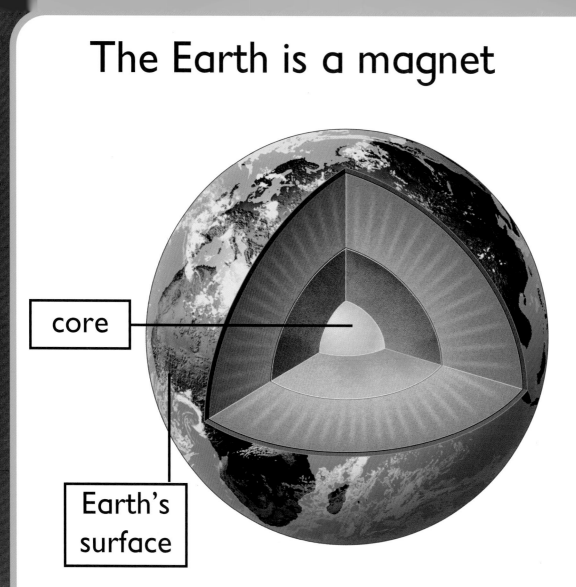

core

Earth's surface

The Earth consists of layers of rock. In the centre is the core. It is made of very heavy iron. This iron core is like an enormous magnet.

The Earth's magnet can be felt by other magnets. The lines show how the Earth's magnet pulls other magnets towards the magnetic **north pole**.

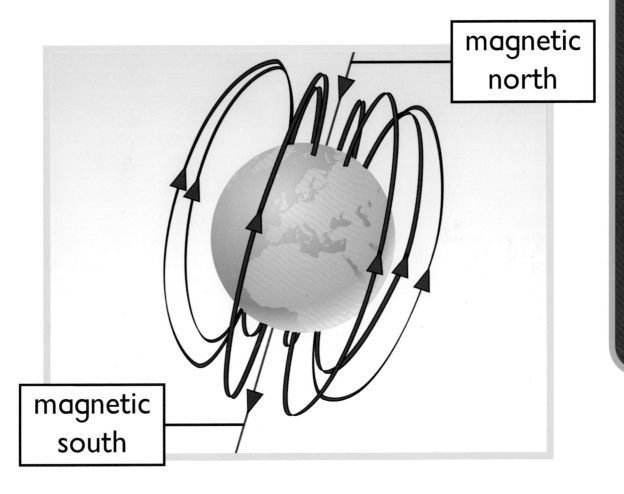

magnetic north

magnetic south

Using the Earth's magnet

This girl is testing the pull of the Earth's magnet. She ties a magnet by a string and lets it swing around.

When the magnet stops swinging, one end points north. The same thing happens every time. Which way does the other end point? (Answer on page 31.)

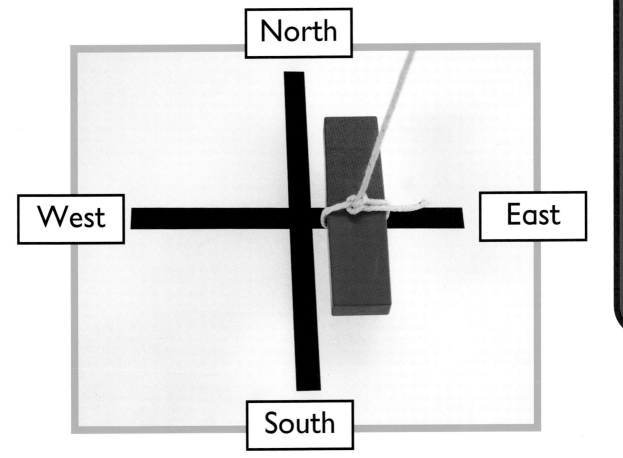

North

West

East

South

Compasses

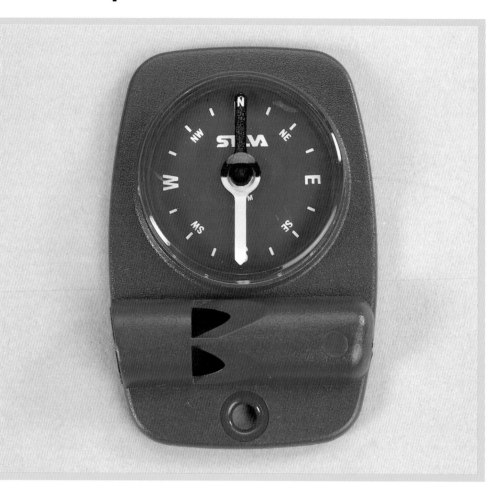

A **compass** is an **instrument** used to find the direction of north. The needle is a small magnet. The rest of the compass is non-magnetic.

Ships and aeroplanes have a compass on them. The pilot of this plane checks the compass. He uses it to fly the plane in the right direction.

Glossary

aluminium a kind of metal that is non-magnetic

cloth fabric that is used to make things like clothes, curtains and sheets

collar something that is worn around the neck

compass an instrument that shows the direction of north

gold a rare metal that is worth a lot of money

instrument tool

lodestone rock that forms a natural magnet

north pole the furthest north that you can go on Earth

paperclip piece of bent metal or plastic that is used to hold sheets of paper together

refrigerator machine that keeps things cold

rubber bendy material that is made from oil or the juice of the rubber tree

wagon big box on wheels that is used to carry things by rail

Answers

page 9
The can sticking to the magnet is made of steel.

page 11
The blue, red, green and yellow paperclips are non-magnetic. Only the silver-coloured paperclips are magnetic.

page 27
The other end of the magnet points to the south.

Index

Titles in the *My World of Science* series include:

Hardback   0 431 13700 5

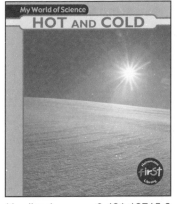

Hardback   0 431 13715 3

Hardback   0 431 13712 9

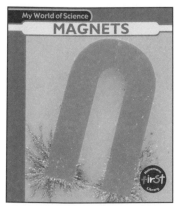

Hardback   0 431 13704 8

Hardback   0 431 13701 3

Hardback   0 431 13702 1

Hardback   0 431 13714 5

Hardback   0 431 13716 1

Hardback   0 431 13703 X

Find out about the other titles in this series on our website www.heinemann.co.uk/library